ESSENTIAL
GUIDE TO THE HOLY BIBLE

MSGR. PIETRO PRINCIPE

ADAPTED FROM THE ORIGINAL
FOR USE IN THE UNITED STATES

D1023700

Libreria Editrice Vaticana

United States Conference of Catholic Bishops
Washington, D.C.

CONTENTS

"The intention of the Holy Spirit is to teach us how to go to heaven, and not how heaven goes."

—Galileo Galilei (1564-1642),
from a letter to Christina of Lorraine,
Grand Duchess of Tuscany

ABBREVIATIONS

Old Testament

Gn	Genesis	Prv	Proverbs
Ex	Exodus	Eccl	Ecclesiastes
Lv	Leviticus	Sg (Song)	Song of Songs
Nm	Numbers	Wis	Wisdom
Dt	Deuteronomy	Sir	Sirach
Jos	Joshua	Is	Isaiah
Jgs	Judges	Jer	Jeremiah
Ru	Ruth	Lam	Lamentations
1 Sm	1 Samuel	Bar	Baruch
2 Sm	2 Samuel	Ez	Ezekiel
1 Kgs	1 Kings	Dn	Daniel
2 Kgs	2 Kings	Hos	Hosea
1 Chr	1 Chronicles	Jl	Joel
2 Chr	2 Chronicles	Am	Amos
Ezr	Ezra	Ob	Obadiah
Neh	Nehemiah	Jon	Jonah
Tb	Tobit	Mi	Micah
Jdt	Judith	Na	Nahum
Est	Esther	Hb	Habakkuk
1 Mc	1 Maccabees	Zep	Zephaniah
2 Mc	2 Maccabees	Hg	Haggai
Jb	Job	Zec	Zechariah
Ps	Psalms	Mal	Malachi

New Testament

Mt	Matthew
Mk	Mark
Lk	Luke
Jn	John
Acts	Acts of the Apostles
Rom	Romans
1 Cor	1 Corinthians
2 Cor	2 Corinthians
Gal	Galatians
Eph	Ephesians
Phil	Philippians
Col	Colossians
1 Thes	1 Thessalonians
2 Thes	2 Thessalonians
1 Tm	1 Timothy
2 Tm	2 Timothy
Ti	Titus
Phlm	Philemon
Heb	Hebrews
Jas	James
1 Pt	1 Peter
2 Pt	2 Peter
1 Jn	1 John
2 Jn	2 John
3 Jn	3 John
Jude	Jude
Rev	Revelation

Other Abbreviations

OT	Old Testament
NT	New Testament
DV	*Dei Verbum*
BC	Before Christ (*Ante Christum*)
AD	After Christ (*Anno Domini*)
LXX	Septuagint, the Greek version of the Old Testament

The Bible and the Internet

Numerous Web sites are dedicated to the Bible. They are an excellent resource for knowing and studying the Word of God.

Some of the main Catholic references are listed below:

www.usccb.org/nab
www.vatican.va/archive/bible
www.bibliaclerus.org

INTRODUCTION

he Bible—the all-time best-selling book, translated into the most languages in the world, as well as the book most heavily commented on—is not easy reading.

Publications about biblical questions, which are numerous and are the product of intensive research by eminent scholars, constitute a cultural source of great interest.

This discussion is limited to several brief and indispensable notions, the ones that Christians cannot do without in order to begin studying the Bible, the **Book of Books**.

Biblical Citations

The ancients usually wrote continuous texts without subdivisions. In order to make consulting the Bible simpler and quicker, the practice of dividing the books into chapters took root during the Middle Ages. These chapters were in turn divided into short phrases called "verses." Each verse was later marked with a little number.

In Bible citations, the name of the book can be abbreviated. The chapter follows, and then the verse number. For example, the citation "Mk 9:2" indicates verse number two of chapter 9 in the Gospel according to Mark. This is a very useful method for quickly finding any phrase in any edition of the Bible.

1. THE BIBLE

- The Book of Books
- An extraordinary story
- An *inspired* Word

The Book of Books

he word "**Bible**," derived from the Greek language, means "**books**": it includes a group of narratives and literary compositions transmitted by the Judeo-Christian tradition, first orally and then in writing.

The term "**Bible**" is of Christian origin, as are the terms "**Old Testament**" and "**New Testament**."

In ancient times, the first writing systems were developed through the use of symbols inscribed in clay and stone. The Egyptians began writing on sheets made from papyrus, a plant that grows in the waters of the Nile. Later, animal skins called **parchments** were also used.

The manuscripts of the Bible on papyrus and parchment were written in Hebrew, Aramaic, and Greek. After the first century, the Church perceived the need for translations of the Bible into Latin: the most famous is known as the *Vetus Latina* (that is, the "Old Latin Bible"). In 382, St. Jerome was directed by Pope Damasus I to write a new translation, which then came to be known as the *Vulgate* (that is, it was spread or "divulged" among the people). After later revisions to the Vulgate by others, the Council of Florence established the Vulgate as authentic in 1442, and the Council of Trent confirmed it in 1546.

The first printed version—called the "Forty-Two–Line Bible"—was completed by Johann Gutenberg on February 23, 1455, in Mainz, Germany.

The first English translation of the Bible dates to the fourteenth century, though portions of the text were translated into Old English as early as the seventh century.

Christians have attributed **different names** to the Bible: Word of God, Sacred Scripture, Old and New Testaments, Old and New Covenants, Sacred Books, Scriptures, Holy Writ, Scripture, Book of Books, the Good Book.

An Extraordinary Story

he Bible is the best-selling book translated into the most languages—roughly 2,500 languages and dialects. It is natural to wonder about the reason for this phenomenon. The reason is not so much the Bible's age as its uniqueness: **God himself speaks through the authors who have written**.

The Bible reveals the mystery of God as the creator of the world and the creator of human beings through an act of love.

This event takes place throughout history by means of words and deeds, which serve to highlight **God's masterpiece, human beings, endowed with** *freedom*. Every person possesses this unique gift.

> **The greatest gift that** in his largess **God**
> Creating **made**, and unto his own goodness
> Nearest conformed, and that which he
> doth prize
>
> Most highly, **is the freedom of the will**,
> Wherewith the creatures of intelligence
> Both all and only were and are endowed.
> (Dante, *Paradiso* V:19-24; emphasis added
> [trans. Henry Wadsworth Longfellow])

Divine omnipotence does not seek to counter the free person's autonomy (what a never-ending human drama!), which has the potential to do good or evil, to accept or reject the Word of God and its love. It is so from the first moment of creation (Gn 2:17).

Human beings have always had the desire to understand the heart of God and to communicate with him: the Bible is the narration of that encounter. "In the sacred books the Father who is in heaven comes lovingly to meet his children, and talks with them" (Second Vatican Council, *Dogmatic Constitution on Divine Revelation* [*Dei Verbum*] [DV],[1] no. 21).

The story of humanity and the story of salvation are rooted in two **historical events: the will of God that creates the universe, and the redemptive act of Christ that saves humanity**. These two events accomplish the wonderful encounter between human reality and divine transcendence.

In the first centuries and subsequently during the Middle Ages, Christian culture, preaching, and formation relied on Sacred Scripture as their primary reference.

---

1 Second Vatican Council, *Dogmatic Constitution on Divine Revelation* (*Dei Verbum*) (DV), in *Vatican Council II: Volume 1: The Conciliar and Post Conciliar Documents*, ed. Austin Flannery (Northport, NY: Costello Publishing, 1996). Subsequent references to this and all other texts of the Second Vatican Council are provided in the text.

In recent centuries, an acute sense of historical criticism emerged in society. That social environment affected the study of the Bible as well. As a result, the *historical-critical method* for the interpretation of the Bible has become widespread among biblical scholars (see sidebar).

Today, we are witnessing an extraordinary flourishing of interest in the Sacred Scriptures for various reasons, but primarily because of the document *Dei Verbum* from the Second Vatican Council.

The Historical-Critical Method

The historical-critical method is an important step in understanding biblical texts.

"[This method] is a historical method, not only because it is applied to ancient texts—in this case, those of the Bible—and studies their significance from a historical point of view, but also and above all because it seeks to shed light upon the historical processes that gave rise to biblical texts, . . . processes that were often complex and involved a long period of time. At the different stages of their production, the texts of the Bible were addressed to various categories of hearers or readers living in different places and different times.

"It is a critical method because, in each of its steps (from textual criticism to redaction criticism [scholarly study of various editions]), it operates with the help of scientific criteria that seek to be as objective as possible. In this way it aims to make accessible to the modern reader the meaning of biblical texts, often very difficult to comprehend.

"As an analytical method, it studies the biblical text in the same fashion as it would study any other ancient text and comments upon it as an expression of human discourse. However, above all in the area of redaction criticism, it does allow the exegete [or Bible scholar] to gain a better grasp of the content of divine revelation."*

---

* Pontifical Biblical Commission, *The Interpretation of the Bible in the Church* (Washington, DC: USCCB, 1994), §I.A.2.

An Inspired Word

or Jews and Christians, the Bible has its origin in God. Catholics speak of *inspiration*, seeking to indicate the specific influence exercised by God on the writers of the biblical books.

For believers, the expressions **"inspiration"** and **"Word of God"** indicate the *divine roots* of the Bible as fundamental criteria for a piece of writing that contains **truths communicated by God** to human beings for the purpose of salvation. "The divinely revealed realities, which are contained and presented in the text of sacred Scripture, have been written down under the inspiration of the Holy Spirit. . . . [Therefore,] we must acknowledge that the books of Scripture, firmly, faithfully and without error, teach that truth which God, for the sake of our salvation, wished to see confided to the sacred Scriptures" (DV, no. 11).

Given all this, for believers, the Bible is the Word of God, and "to compose the sacred books, God chose certain men who, all the while he employed them in this task, made full use of their powers and faculties" (DV, no. 11).

The Languages Used

The Bible was written in three languages: Hebrew, Aramaic, and Greek.

Except for a few texts, the entire Old Testament was written in **Hebrew**: a Semitic language written from right to left. Hebrew has only twenty-two consonants and no vowels. With its limited vocabulary, Hebrew does not have superlatives. (For example, the concept of "holiest" is expressed by repeating the word "holy" three times.)

Aramaic—the common language of Palestinian Jews in the time of Jesus—is limited to certain parts of the Old Testament.

All of the books of the New Testament were written in **Greek**.

Some fragments of the Bible exist in other ancient languages as well.

In the fourth century BC, Alexander the Great (356-323) imposed the Greek language on Palestine. Thus, even the Hebrew Scriptures were translated into Greek, which was used in daily conversation. This translation is known as the "Septuagint" ("LXX") because, according to legend, seventy Hebrew scholars—isolated in separate cells—each wrote an individual translation, and all of them miraculously turned out to be identical. This translation was commonly used in the early Church.

2. THE BOOKS OF THE BIBLE

- The Canon of Holy Books
- The Old Testament
- The New Testament

The Canon of Holy Books

he narratives, poems, songs, genealogies, and other types of writing that are in the Bible have ancient roots in both Judaism and Christianity. They were passed down orally before being collected and written down. They were composed over a period of a thousand years. No biblical book was composed after the beginning of the second century AD.

The books were gradually collected through a long selective process applied by the community. By the end of the fourth century the Church arrived at common agreement concerning the "canon": that is, the official list of scriptural texts believed to contain the inspired word of God. These books were included in St. Jerome's Vulgate. The *canon of the*

New Testament began to be formed from the beginning of Christianity. "By means of the same Tradition the full canon of the sacred books is known" (DV, no. 8).

The living Tradition is the *link* between the person of Christ and the sacred writings. It transmits what Jesus said and did. This *deposit* of revealed truths has always accompanied the community of believers since the time of the Apostles.

The oldest list of the Holy Books of which we are aware is the *Muratorian Fragment* (published by L. A. Muratori in 1740), which dates back to the second century AD.

Scripture and Tradition in Divine Revelation

Tradition is the living transmission of the message of the Gospel in the Church. The oral preaching of the Apostles, and the written message of salvation under the inspiration of the Holy Spirit (the Bible), are conserved and handed on as the Deposit of Faith through the apostolic succession in the Church. Both the living Tradition and the written Scriptures have their common source in the Revelation of God in Jesus Christ.

The Old Testament

any scholars maintain that oral traditions about the salvation of the People of God began to be set in writing toward the end of the tenth century BC.

The ways and periods in which the Sacred Scriptures were composed still require lengthy and laborious research by scholars to this day.

After the destruction of Jerusalem (AD 70), the influential rabbinical School of Jamnia helped to finalize the Jewish canon of Scripture, setting the twenty-four books that would come to form the Old Testament.

The Church Fathers based the canon on the Septuagint (see sidebar "The Languages Used," in previous section), which divided the books differently and contained more writings. Catholics have forty-six books in the Old Testament (Protestants have thirty-nine).

The books of the Old Testament are typically presented in particular literary subdivisions.

The **first five books** are known as the *Pentateuch*. They are followed by the *historical*, *wisdom*, and *prophetic* books.

The collection of Old Testament writings is normally classified by Catholics into the following order.

Pentateuch (Torah)

Genesis (Gn)
The word "genesis" comes from the Greek and means "origins." The book recounts the origins of the universe and of human beings in simple, figurative language. Genesis is the starting point of Revelation and shows the human race's need for salvation. This book recounts the stories of Adam, Eve, Abel, Cain, Noah, Abraham, Sarah, Hagar, Isaac, Jacob, and his children.

Exodus (Ex)
This Greek title means "departure." The book recounts how the descendants of the Patriarchs—who are talked about in Genesis—were taken out of Egypt under the guidance of Moses. Exodus is of fundamental importance: Israel becomes witness to the One God, from whom Moses receives the Decalogue (the Ten Commandments).

Leviticus (Lv)
The title of this book, which is dedicated almost exclusively to laws, indicates the duties of the priests of Israel, who belonged to the Tribe of Levi. In this book, our need to honor God through external worship, and not just through interior worship, becomes apparent.

Numbers (Nm)

This book continues the narration of the Exodus of Israel toward the Promised Land. The protagonists are Moses; Aaron, his brother; and Joshua, his future successor. The book describes the curious story of Balaam—a renowned seer—and his donkey, which speaks to its master and admonishes him.

Deuteronomy (Dt)

This title means "second law." This book retells the events of the Exodus from a different perspective. They are presented through a collection of three speeches that Moses addressed to Israel before entering into the Promised Land.

Historical Books

Joshua (Jos)

This book takes its title from the protagonist, who led Israel into the Promised Land after the death of Moses. It tells how the children of Israel took possession of the land of Canaan, including the Battle of Jericho.

Judges (Jgs)

The judges were military and political leaders. This book recounts the history of Israel from the death of

Joshua to the anointing of Saul as king. It includes familiar stories, such as the famous story of Samson and Delilah.

Ruth (Ru)

The protagonist is a Moabite (a foreigner and enemy of Israel) who nonetheless becomes part of the family tree of Jesus by marrying Boaz and giving birth to Obed (the father of Jesse and grandfather of David). The book portrays the love and loyalty of human beings in working their way through tragic circumstances toward participation in the community of the faithful People of God.

First Book of Samuel (1 Sm)

Samuel is the first major prophetic figure and the last judge. This book, written by an unknown author, recounts the tragic ordeals of Saul, the first king of Israel. Saul fought against the Philistines, who would only later be defeated by the shepherd David, who managed to kill the giant Goliath.

Second Book of Samuel (2 Sm)

This book is almost entirely dedicated to the reign of the powerful figure of King David, including his successes (moving the Ark of the Covenant to Jerusalem) and his failures (his sin with Bathsheba).

First Book of Kings (1 Kgs)

The entire narrative deals with Solomon, the son of King David and Bathsheba. Anointed as king, he shone with wisdom. The construction of the Temple of Jerusalem began under him, and he is known for his wise verdict in the case of a child claimed by two mothers.

Second Book of Kings (2 Kgs)

In this book, the tumultuous events following the death of Solomon lead to the division of the united kingdom into Israel in the north and Judah in the south. The book tells the stories of important individuals such as Elijah and Elisha. It concludes with the catastrophic conquest of Jerusalem and the exile of the Chosen People to Babylon.

First Book of Chronicles (1 Chr)

This book presents a new description of the history of the People of God. The author, known only as "the Chronicler," begins with Adam and recounts the history of the people up to the time of David. The book underscores the status of Jerusalem and its divinely established Temple worship as the center of religious life for the Jewish people.

Second Book of Chronicles (2 Chr)

This book resumes the history with the merits of Solomon and then turns its attention to the kings of Judah, giving little attention to the northern kingdom of Israel. The conclusion presents the decree by King Cyrus of Persia regarding the return to Jerusalem from exile and the rebuilding of the Temple.

Ezra (Ezr)

The protagonist is an important priest-scribe who returns to Jerusalem from Babylon during the reign of King Artaxerxes I of Persia. The king authorizes Ezra to appoint magistrates and administer justice in Israel. Known for being well versed in the Law, Ezra built a community characterized by fidelity to the Torah, Judaism's authentic way of life.

Nehemiah (Neh)

This book narrates the memories of Nehemiah as the governor sent to Judah by King Artaxerxes I of Persia. A contemporary of Ezra, he rebuilt the walls of Jerusalem.

Tobit (Tb)

This book recounts a folk story of a pious Jewish man, Tobit, and his son, Tobiah. Its narrative and wisdom sayings are rich with teachings that encourage trust in God's Providence.

Judith (Jdt)

This book tells the story of a Jewish widow named Judith. Known for her beauty and her piety, Judith kills Holofernes, one of the leaders under the Assyrian king, by cutting off his head, thereby saving her community.

Esther (Est)

This book tells another story of the deliverance of the Jewish people. Esther charms Ahasuerus, the Persian king, and becomes queen and protector of Israel. She intervenes in a plot by the wicked minister Haman to destroy the Jewish people. After the Jewish people rout the attack, Haman is hanged instead of Mordecai, a kinsman of Esther, who had been unjustly slandered. The Jewish feast of Purim has its origin in these events.

First Book of Maccabees (1 Mc)

The heroes of the book, who lived in the second century BC, are the members of a family who lead an insurrection against the king of Syria and his successors. The contest described in the book is a struggle, not simply between Jew and Gentile, but between those who would uphold the law and those, Jews or Gentiles, who would destroy it. Both First and Second Maccabees describe the rededication of the Temple, the origin of the Jewish feast of Hanukkah.

Second Book of Maccabees (2 Mc)
This book is not a sequel to the First Book of Maccabees, but it recounts many of the same episodes, focusing on the figure of Judas Maccabeus. This book contains important theological teachings on the resurrection of the just on the last day, the intercession of the saints in heaven for people living on earth, and the power of the living to offer prayers and sacrifices for the dead.

Wisdom Books

Job (Jb)
A wise and rich God-fearing shepherd is put to the test by Satan. The poetic text, considered a literary masterpiece, deals with the mystery of God and the suffering of the innocent.

Psalms (Ps)

These characteristic lyrical songs were most likely composed for liturgical worship. There are 150 of them in a variety of literary styles (praise, lamentation, penitence, etc.). Many of them are attributed to King David. They are writings of great intensity and lyricism. It has been rightly said that the Psalms are "a school of prayer." They not only provide us with models to follow but inspire us to voice our own deepest feelings and aspirations.

Why Does the Numbering of the Psalms Differ in Various Translations of the Bible?

The Hebrew Psalter, or Book of Psalms, numbers 150 songs. The corresponding number in the Septuagint differs because of a different division and combiing of certain psalms. For this reason, the numbering in the Greek Psalter (which was followed by the Latin Vulgate) is usually one digit behind the Hebrew. In the *New American Bible* and most other modern English translations, the numbering of the psalms and verses follows the Hebrew numbering. Some Catholic liturgical texts follow the Greek numbering and put the Hebrew numbering in parentheses.

Proverbs (Prv)

This book of sayings or maxims of wisdom includes brief and effective phrases about fear of God and about his laws. Proverbs concentrates on Wisdom itself, treating it as a virtually independent entity and personifying it as an attractive woman. Other books urge readers to perform wise acts, but Proverbs urges them to seek Wisdom itself. The book ends with a hymn praising a virtuous woman.

Ecclesiastes (Eccl)

Also known as *Qoheleth* in Hebrew, this title can be translated as "assembler" (of students, listeners) or "collector" (of wisdom sayings). The book confronts the mystery of human life in its daily paradoxes. The book's honest and blunt appraisal of the human condition provides a healthy corrective to the occasionally excessive self-assurance of other wisdom writers. Its radical skepticism is somewhat tempered by the resigned conclusions to rejoice in whatever gifts God may give.

Song of Songs (Song)

The Song of Songs is an exquisite collection of love lyrics, arranged to tell a dramatic tale of mutual desire and courtship. It presents an inspired portrayal of ideal human love. Jewish and Christian traditions across the centuries have adopted allegorical interpretations. The Song is seen as a beautiful picture of the ideal Israel, the Chosen People whom the Lord leads by degrees to a greater understanding and closer union in the bond of perfect love. Christian writers, particularly Origen and St. Bernard, have interpreted the Song in terms of the union between Christ and the Church and of the union between Christ and the individual soul.

Wisdom (Wis)
This writing is the work of a Jew who lived in Alexandria, Egypt, probably during the first century BC. The chronologically last book of the Old Testament, Wisdom stresses the greatness of the ways of wisdom in contrast to the ways of impiety.

Sirach (Sir)
Also known as the "Wisdom of Ben Sira," this book was called "*Liber Ecclesiasticus*" because it was used in the early days of the Church for teaching catechumens. The book contains numerous well-crafted maxims, dealing with a variety of subjects such as the individual, the family, and the community in their relations with one another and with God. The last section of the book recalls the major figures of the Old Testament.

Prophetic Books

Some important individuals are called "Prophets," intermediaries between God and the community who are called to proclaim the Word of God. They are men of God and indicate—at a given time in the history of the Chosen People—the path that God wants for Israel. The prophetic books bear the names of the four major and twelve minor Prophets, in addition to Lamentations and Baruch. The terms "major" and "minor" refer merely to the length of the respective compositions and not to any distinction in the prophetic office.

Isaiah (Is)

One of the greatest writers in the Bible, Isaiah proclaims the need for the Chosen People to have faith. He constantly calls his people back to a reliance on God's promises and away from vain attempts to find security in human plans and intrigues. This vision also leads him to insist on the ethical behavior that is required of human beings who wish to live in the presence of such a holy God. This book includes the four Songs of the Servant of the Lord, applied to Christ throughout Christian tradition.

Jeremiah (Jer)

A harsh messenger for penance, Jeremiah predicted the divine castigation of Israel and witnessed the destruction of the holy city of Jerusalem. Arrest, imprisonment, and public disgrace were his lot. In the nation's apostasy Jeremiah saw the sealing of its doom. He gave voice to the suffering and the hope of the Chosen People.

Lamentations (Lam)

The Book of Lamentations is a collection of five poems that serve as an anguished response to the destruction of Jerusalem in 587 BC, after a long siege by the invading Babylonian army. With its unsparing focus on destruction, pain, and suffering, the book serves an invaluable function as part of Scripture, witnessing to a biblical faith determined to express honestly the harsh realities of a violent world and providing contemporary readers with the language to do the same.

Baruch (Bar)

This book, set during the exile in Babylon, attempts to explain the trauma of the exile in terms of a cycle of sin, punishment, repentance, and return. The prayer of the exiles is a confession of sin and a request for mercy. Following a hymn in praise of Wisdom, a poetic text offers encouragement to the exiles in view of their eventual return. The book concludes with a polemic against idolatry.

Ezekiel (Ez)

After Ezekiel was sent into exile in 597 BC, his first prophetic task was to prepare his fellow countrymen in Babylon for the final destruction of Jerusalem. Accordingly, the first part of the book reproaches Israel for past and present sins and predicts further devastation and a more general exile. After the destruction, Ezekiel's prophecy is characterized by the promise of salvation in a New Covenant. The famous vision of the dry bones in chapter 37 expresses his firm belief in a forthcoming restoration. Ultimately, whatever God does to or for us is motivated by zeal for his own holy name. The new heart and the new spirit that must exist under the New Covenant cannot be the work of man; they too must be the work of God.

Daniel (Dn)

This book takes its name not from the author, but from its hero, among the first Jews deported to Babylon. This work was composed during the bitter persecution carried on by Antiochus IV Epiphanes (167-164 BC) and was written to strengthen and comfort the Jewish people in their ordeal. The book contains traditional stories (chapters 1-6) that tell of the trials and triumphs of the wise Daniel and his three companions. The moral is that people of faith can resist temptation and conquer adversity. The Book of Daniel includes such well-known episodes as the writing on the wall, Daniel in the lion's den, and the story of Susanna, who was freed from the false accusations of the wicked elders.

Hosea (Hos)
The main theme of this book is the infidelity of Israel, who adores false gods, with consequent moral and political disorder. The prophet describes his marriage as a symbol of the covenant between the Lord and Israel, comparing the infidelity of Israel with that of his adulterous wife. Writing approximately two hundred years before the Song of Songs, Hosea began the Old Testament tradition of describing the relation between the Lord and Israel in terms of marriage.

Joel (Jl)
This prophecy is rich in apocalyptic imagery and strongly eschatological in tone. It was composed about 400 BC. Its prevailing theme is the day of the Lord.

Amos (Am)

A man of the desert, Amos stigmatizes the solely external worship of the Jewish people, who were living in social and religious corruption. He calls the people back to the high moral and religious demands of the Lord's Revelation. Amos's message stands as one of the most powerful voices ever to challenge hypocrisy and injustice.

Obadiah (Ob)

This is the shortest book of the entire Old Testament. The prophecy is a bitter cry for vengeance against Edom for its pride and its crimes. Mount Esau in Edom will be occupied and ravaged by the enemy, while through the might of the Lord, Mount Zion will be restored to its former sanctity and security.

Jonah (Jon)

This account tells the story of the disobedient prophet Jonah, who remains three days and three nights in the belly of a large fish before accepting the task of calling Nineveh, the capital of the Assyrian empire, to conversion. This fascinating story caricatures a narrow mentality that would see God's interest extending only to Israel, whereas God is presented as concerned with and merciful to even the inhabitants of Nineveh.

Micah (Mi)

A contemporary of Isaiah, Micah attacked rich exploiters of the poor, fraudulent merchants, venal judges, and corrupt priests and prophets. Through the prophet, the Lord announces the impending punishment of God's people, by means of military defeat and exile, because of their failure to establish justice. After that punishment, God will bring the people back to their land and establish perpetual peace. This prophecy foretells the birth of the Messiah in Bethlehem.

Nahum (Na)

This book prophesies the destruction of Nineveh by the Babylonians. Nahum asserts God's moral government of the world. Nineveh's doom is evidence that God stands against oppression and the abuse of power. Thus, Nineveh's demise is viewed as an act of divine justice.

Habakkuk (Hb)

A contemporary of Jeremiah, Habakkuk is the only prophet to devote his entire work to the question of the justice of God's government of the world. Habakkuk's challenge is set up as a dialogue between the prophet and God, in which Habakkuk's complaints about injustices are followed by God's promises that the perpetrators will be punished, assuring the prophet of the reliability of God's rule and calling for human faithfulness.

Zephaniah (Zep)

Zephaniah's prophecy of judgment on Judah and Jerusalem emphasizes, perhaps more than any other prophecy, the devastation and death that divine judgment will bring. Described as the day of the Lord, the Day of Judgment is pictured as a time of darkness, of anguish and distress, of destruction and plunder of cities, and of threat to all life, human and animal alike. The major sins motivating this judgment, in Zephaniah's view, are Judah's worship of other deities and its unjust and abusive leadership.

Haggai (Hg)

The prophet encourages the repatriated Jews after the exile in Babylon, despite the destruction of the Temple. The prophet links the well-being of the community to the work of Temple restoration. The period of Haggai's ministry marks the resumption of work on the Temple, the symbol of divine presence among the people.

Zechariah (Zec)

The prophet Zechariah promotes the work of rebuilding the Temple and encourages the returned exiles, especially their leaders. He portrays the messianic future under the figure of a prosperous land to which the nations come in pilgrimage, eager to follow the God of Israel.

Malachi (Mal)

Malachi foresees the time when all nations will offer a pure oblation. The day of the Lord is coming. But first the forerunner must prepare the soil for repentance and true worship. When the ground is prepared, God will appear, measuring out rewards and punishments and purifying the nation in the furnace of judgment. He will create a new order in which the ultimate triumph of good is inevitable.

The Sacred Books of the Jews

Judaism traditionally uses three subdivisions when referring to the Scriptures:

- The **Law** (Torah): Genesis, Exodus, Leviticus, Numbers, Deuteronomy
- The **Prophets** (Nevi'im):
  - The early Prophets (before the Babylonian exile, 587 BC)—Joshua, Judges, Samuel (1 and 2 together), Kings (1 and 2 together)
  - The later Prophets (containing messages scattered throughout the history of Israel)—Isaiah, Jeremiah, Ezekiel, and the twelve Prophets: Hosea, Joel, Amos, Obadiah, Jonah, Micah, Nahum, Habakkuk, Zephaniah, Haggai, Zechariah, Malachi
- The **Writings** (Ketuvim): Psalms, Proverbs, Job, Song of Songs, Ruth, Lamentations, Ecclesiastes, Esther, Daniel, Ezra-Nehemiah (together), Chronicles (1 and 2 together)

Jews do not refer to their Scriptures as "the Bible." Instead, they use the word "**Tanakh**," an acronym formed from the three Hebrew words *Torah*, *Nevi'im*, and *Ketuvim*.

Qumran and the Dead Sea Scrolls

In the spring of 1947, various manuscripts of great interest were found in several caves near a place called Qumran, to the northwest of the Dead Sea. During the war with Rome (before AD 70), a Jewish community hid the scrolls—some of which were already two hundred years old at that time—in the caves. Many scrolls contain books of the Bible: a complete scroll of Isaiah, and other fragments of the Hebrew Bible. In addition, many biblical and parabiblical passages and fragments came to light. These manuscripts are commonly referred to as the "Dead Sea Scrolls."

Since their discovery, the debates among scholars concerning these texts have been endless.

Studying them is of significant interest in order to understand the environment in which the Christian faith developed and to identify the oldest existing editions of the biblical books.

The New Testament

nd the Word became flesh" (Jn 1:14). God "sent his Son, the eternal Word who enlightens all" (DV, no. 4).

So begins the story that we Christians call the New Testament. All of the sacred writings composed during the time of the Apostles are grouped under this heading.

Jesus did not write anything. In order to be true followers of him, we need only listen to his Word in the Tradition and in the Sacred Scriptures and to practice his teachings. Even an illiterate person who wishes to believe can follow him.

After the Resurrection, the disciples of Jesus began spreading his Word to the world. The book of the Acts of the Apostles reconstructs the history of the early Christian communities, which—first through oral preaching and then later with writings—announced the *message of salvation*, the *Gospel* (*Good News*), wishing to transmit what they had personally seen and experienced.

Initially, several accounts of the events of the life of Jesus were written down: a collection of parables, a little book of miracles, the story of the Passion. These compositions, distributed among the community of believers, were used in the collecting and editing of the Acts of the Apostles and the four Gospels.

This transmission of events and writings dating back to the Apostles has become enriched over time, spreading knowledge of the sacred books among Christians. "By means of the same Tradition the full canon of the sacred books is known" (DV, no. 8).

In the Christian Bible, the books of the New Testament are ordered as follows.

Gospel According to Matthew (Mt)

Traditionally, the first Gospel was attributed to Matthew (also known as Levi). Jesus sees him and wants Matthew to follow him, taking him away from his profession as a tax collector. The position of the Gospel according to Matthew as the first of the four Gospels reflects the high esteem in which the Church holds it. This Gospel serves as a bridge from the Old Testament to the New Testament with its concern for "fulfillment." Matthew dedicates particular attention to the Church founded by Christ on Peter. His Gospel includes the well-known Sermon on the Mount (chapters 5-7).

Gospel According to Mark (Mk)

The shortest of all New Testament Gospels, the Gospel according to Mark was likely the first to have been written. It often tells of Jesus' ministry in more detail than either Matthew or Luke. It recounts what

Jesus did in a vivid style, where one incident follows directly upon another. Mark's Gospel reflects themes common in the preaching of Peter and Paul. Mark stresses Jesus' message about the Kingdom of God that now breaks into human life as Good News, and about Jesus himself as being the Gospel of God. Jesus is the Son whom God has sent to rescue humanity by serving and by sacrificing his life.

Gospel According to Luke (Lk)

Early Christian tradition, from the late second century on, identifies the author both of this Gospel and of the Acts of the Apostles as being Luke, a Syrian from Antioch, who is mentioned in several of Paul's letters. No gospel writer is more concerned than Luke with the mercy and compassion of Jesus, with the role of the Spirit in the life of Jesus and of the Christian disciple, with the importance of prayer, or with Jesus' concern for women. Luke's Gospel tells the story of Jesus' birth in Bethlehem and includes such well-known parables as the Prodigal Son and the Good Samaritan.

These first three Gospels are known as synoptic, *a Greek word meaning "shared view," because they present parallel accounts.*

Historical Sources

Jesus existed historically. Three types of sources testify to this fact:

1. **Christian sources**
   - Letters of St. Paul (AD 51-65)
   - Synoptic Gospels (AD 65-75)
   - Acts of the Apostles (AD 80)
   - Gospel according to John (AD 100)

2. **Judaic sources**
   - Flavius Josephus (first century AD)
   - Mishnah (second century AD)
   - Talmud (fifth century AD)

3. **Pagan sources**
   - Pliny the Younger (around AD 112)
   - Tacitus (around AD 117)
   - Suetonius (around AD 120)

Gospel According to John (Jn)

The Gospel according to John is quite different in character from the three synoptic Gospels. It is highly literary and symbolic. It does not follow the same order or reproduce the same stories as the synoptic Gospels. It is the product of a developed theological reflection, probably written in the last decade of the first century AD. The narrative contains a series of "signs"—the Gospel's word for the wondrous deeds of Jesus. The whole Gospel of John is a progressive revelation of the glory of God's only Son, who comes to reveal the Father and then returns in glory to the Father. It includes such events as the wedding at Cana, the Samaritan woman at the well, and the raising of Lazarus, as well as the discourse on the Bread of Life and the farewell discourse at the Last Supper.

Acts of the Apostles (Acts)

This book, the second volume from the evangelist Luke, describes the development of the Church at its beginning, through the work of the Apostles and particularly of Peter and Paul. In the development of the Church from a Jewish Christian origin in Jerusalem to a series of Christian communities among the Gentiles of the Roman Empire, Luke perceives the action of God in history laying open the heart of all humanity to the divine message of salvation. Under the guidance of the Holy Spirit, the Good News spreads around the world.

Letter to the Romans (Rom)

Of all the letters of Paul, the Letter to the Romans has long held pride of place. It is the longest of the Apostle's letters and expounds upon the Gospel of God's righteousness that saves all who believe. Paul's Letter to the Romans is a powerful exposition of the doctrine of the supremacy of Christ and of faith in Christ as the source of salvation. It is an implicit plea to the Christians at Rome, and to all Christians, to hold fast to that faith.

First Letter to the Corinthians (1 Cor)

Paul's first letter to the Church in Corinth provides us with insight into the life of an early Christian community. Through it we can glimpse both the strengths and the weaknesses of this small group in Corinth, a great city of the ancient world: a group of men and women who have accepted the Good News of Christ and are now trying to realize in their lives the implications of their Baptism. Certain passages of the letter are important for the understanding of early Christian teaching on the Eucharist, on the resurrection of the body, and on marriage and celibacy.

Second Letter to the Corinthians (2 Cor)

The Second Letter to the Corinthians is the most personal of all of Paul's writings, and it reveals much about his character. In it he deals with crises that have arisen in the Corinthian church. The importance of the issues at stake between them calls forth from him an enormous effort of personal persuasion, as well as doctrinal considerations that are of great value. Paul's interpretation of Exodus in chapter 3 offers a striking example of early apologetic use of the Old Testament. Paul reveals his faith that Jesus' Passion and Resurrection are the pattern for all Christian life, and he expresses a spirituality of ministry unsurpassed in the New Testament.

Letter to the Galatians (Gal)

The new Christians whom Paul is addressing are converts from paganism who are now being enticed by other missionaries to add the observances of the Jewish law, including the rite of circumcision, to the Cross of Christ as a means of salvation. When Paul learned of the situation, he wrote this defense of his apostolic authority and of the correct understanding of the faith. He sets forth the unique importance of Christ and his redemptive sacrifice on the Cross, the freedom that Christians enjoy from the old burdens of the law, the total sufficiency of Christ and of faith in Christ as the way to God and to eternal life, and the beauty of the new life of the Spirit. Galatians is thus a summary of basic Pauline theology.

Letter to the Ephesians (Eph)

Possibly written from prison in Rome, Paul's Letter to the Ephesians is the great Pauline letter about the Church. It deals, however, not so much with a congregation in the city of Ephesus in Asia Minor as with the worldwide Church, the head of which is Christ, the purpose of which is to be the instrument for making God's plan of salvation known throughout the universe. Yet this ecclesiology is anchored in God's saving love, shown in Jesus Christ; and the whole of redemption is rooted in the plan and accomplishment of the Triune God.

Letter to the Philippians (Phil)

Written while Paul was imprisoned, this beautiful letter is rich in insights into Paul's theology and into his apostolic love and concern for the Gospel and his converts. Paul reveals his human sensitivity and tenderness, his enthusiasm for Christ as the key to life and death, and his deep feeling for those Christians who dwell in Philippi. With them he shares his hopes and convictions, his anxieties and fears, revealing the total confidence in Christ that constitutes faith. The letter incorporates a hymn about the salvation that

God has brought about through Christ, applied by Paul to the relations of Christians with one another. The Letter to the Philippians has been termed "the letter of joy."

Letter to the Colossians (Col)

In this letter, Paul affirms that Christ possesses the sum total of redemptive power and that the spiritual renewal of the human person occurs through contact in Baptism with the person of Christ, who died and rose. True Christian asceticism consists in the conquering of personal sins and in the practice of love of neighbor, in accordance with the standard set by Christ.

First Letter to the Thessalonians (1 Thes)

Most scholars consider this letter to be the earliest written document of the New Testament, dating to around AD 50-51—earlier even than the Gospels. In this letter, Paul's optimism regarding the Thessalonians' spiritual welfare is tempered by his insistence on their recognition of the selfless love shown by the missionaries. Paul emphasizes not only the content of his Gospel but also his manner of presenting it, for both attest to God's grace as freely bestowed and powerfully carried out. It is a letter of hope, since those who have died share in the Resurrection of Christ. Specific principles for acting morally stem from one's relationship to God through Christ by the sending of the Holy Spirit. Thus, moral conduct is the practical, personal expression of one's Christian faith, love, and hope.

Second Letter to the Thessalonians (2 Thes)

Paul's second letter speaks of the Thessalonians' increasing faith and love in the face of outside persecution. The heart of the letter deals with a problem threatening the faith of the community. A message involving a prophetic oracle and apparently a forged letter about the coming of the day of the Lord has upset the life of the Thessalonian church. The letter describes what will happen at the Lord's coming and offers prayers for divine strength. The closing part of the letter deals with lifestyles and with correction of disorderly elements within the community.

First Letter to Timothy (1 Tm)

Timothy, whom Paul converted, was of mixed Jewish and Gentile parentage. He was the apostle's companion on Paul's second and third missionary journeys and was often sent by him on special missions. The central passage of the letter expresses the principal motive that should guide Timothy's conduct in leading the Christian community in Ephesus: preservation of the purity of the Church's doctrine against false teaching.

Second Letter to Timothy (2 Tm)

This letter is more personal than the First Letter to Timothy. It addresses Timothy in vivid terms and depicts Paul's courage and hope in the face of discouragements late in the course of his apostolic ministry. The letter takes on the character of a final exhortation and testament from Paul to the younger Timothy and offers Timothy, as a motive for steadfastness, Paul's own example of firmness in faith despite adverse circumstances.

Letter to Titus (Ti)

Paul addresses this letter to Titus as being the person in charge of developing the Church on the large Mediterranean island of Crete. The letter discusses topics of church life and structure: presbyter-bishops, groups with which one must work in the Church, and admonitions for conduct based on the grace and love of God that appeared in Jesus Christ. The warmer personal tone of the Second Letter to Timothy is here replaced by emphasis on church office and on how to live in the society of the day, in which deceivers and heretics abound.

Letter to Philemon (Phlm)

Paul wrote this short letter while in prison. It concerns Onesimus, a slave who has run away from his master. Onesimus has been converted to Christ by Paul. Paul sends him back to his master, Philemon, with this letter asking that he be welcomed willingly by his old master not just as a slave but as a brother in Christ. Paul's letter deals with an accepted institution of antiquity, human slavery. But Paul breathes into this letter the spirit of Christ and of equality within the Christian community.

Letter to the Hebrews (Heb)

The main theme of this letter—the author of which is unknown—is the everlasting priesthood of Christ, a priesthood that fulfills the promise of the Old Testament. It also provides the meaning God ultimately intended in the sacrifices of the Old Testament: these pointed to the unique sacrifice of Christ, which alone obtains forgiveness of sins. Another important theme of the letter is that of the pilgrimage of the People of God to the heavenly Jerusalem.

In addition to the thirteen letters attributed to Paul plus the Letter to the Hebrews, the New Testament contains seven other letters. Three of these are attributed to John, two to Peter, and one each to James and

Jude. These seven are called the "catholic letters." The reason for the label "catholic," which means "universal," is the perception that these letters—unlike those of Paul, which are directed to a particular local church—are addressed more generally to the universal Church.

Letter of James (Jas)

This letter is an exhortation, concerned almost exclusively with ethical conduct. James emphasizes sound teaching and responsible moral behavior. Ethical norms are derived not primarily from Christology, as in Paul's teachings, but from a concept of salvation that involves conversion, Baptism, forgiveness of sin, and expectation of judgment.

First Letter of Peter (1 Pt)

In this letter, Peter encourages Christians to remain faithful to their standards of belief and conduct in spite of threats of persecution. The suffering and death of Christ serve as both a source of salvation and an example. The letter mingles moral exhortation with catechetical summaries of mercies in Christ. Peter's encouragement to fidelity in spite of suffering is based upon a vision of the meaning of Christian existence, with an emphasis on Baptism.

Second Letter of Peter (2 Pt)

In this second letter, Peter includes both positive teachings and earnest warnings. He seeks to strengthen readers in faith, hope for the future, knowledge, love, and other virtues. This aim is carried out especially by his warning against false teachers. The letter is concerned that Christians not be led into error, but instead grow in grace and knowledge of Jesus Christ.

First Letter of John (1 Jn)

The purpose of this letter—traditionally attributed to the evangelist John—is to combat certain false ideas, especially about Jesus, and to deepen the spiritual and social awareness of the Christian community. Some former members of the community were refusing to acknowledge Jesus as the Christ and were denying that he was a true man. In this letter, the author rejects these theological errors by appealing to the reality and continuity of the apostolic witness to Jesus. The author affirms that authentic Christian love, ethics, and faith take place only within the historical revelation and sacrifice of Jesus Christ. The fullness of Christian life as fellowship with the Father must be based on true belief and must result in charitable living; knowledge of God and love for one another are inseparable, and error in one area inevitably affects the other.

Second Letter of John (2 Jn)

This brief letter is not a theological treatise but a reply to problems within the Church. The themes of love and truth support practical advice on Christian living. The writer encourages community members to show their Christianity by adhering to the great Commandment of mutual love and to the historical truth about Jesus.

Third Letter of John (3 Jn)

Addressed to a pious and generous layman, this letter aims to secure hospitality and material support for missionaries. It is an exhortation to practice hospitality.

Letter of Jude (Jude)

This letter, addressed to all Christians, warns against false teachers.

Revelation (Rev)

The Greek term *"apokalypsis"* means "revelation." The Book of Revelation, rich with symbols, offers not so much a pessimistic view of history as a *cry of hope*: hope in the victory of Christ in the vicissitudes of the world. It is an exhortation to stand firm in the faith, despite the threat of adversity and martyrdom.

The triumph of God in the world of men and women remains a mystery, to be accepted in faith and longed for in hope. It is a triumph that has unfolded in the history of Jesus of Nazareth and continues to unfold in the history of the individual Christian who follows the way of the Cross, even, if necessary, to a martyr's death.

The Apocryphal Books

A series of religious writings that *did not become part of the canon* of the Scriptures are known as "apocryphal" (from the Greek meaning "hidden away").

Some of the apocryphal books of the Old Testament include a Life of Adam and Eve, the Book of Jubilees, the Apocalypse of Moses, the Psalms of Solomon, the Book of Enoch, and the Assumption of Moses.

Apocryphal books of the New Testament include the Epistle of Barnabas, the Book of Hermas entitled "The Shepherd," the Letter of St. Paul to Seneca the Younger, many false Gospels (Gospels of Judas, Mary, Philip, and Thomas), and various Apocalypses (of Mary, Paul, etc.), which feed the imaginations of novelists and cinematographers.

Several of the books that the Catholic Church lists in the canon are considered apocryphal by Protestants because they are not included in the Hebrew Scriptures, though Hebrew texts of some of these books were found at Qumran (see sidebar "Qumran and the Dead Sea Scrolls"). The Jews developed their own canon, which differs from the Old Testament used by the Church Fathers in both the number and order of the books.

During the Reformation, Martin Luther argued that the Jewish canon was more authentic, thereby leading to the differences between "Catholic" and "Protestant" Bibles. However, from its earliest centuries, the Church has taught that these apocryphal books were inspired by the Holy Spirit and are rightly part of the canon. Called "deuterocanonical" by Catholics (from the Greek meaning "second canon"), these books are Tobit, Judith, 1 and 2 Maccabees, Wisdom, Sirach, and Baruch, as well as additions to the books of Daniel and Esther.

3. Some Key Persons in the Bible

Adam
In the account of Genesis, Adam is the first man, whom God has created in his image. He is cast out of the earthly paradise along with Eve. He is the father of Cain and Abel. Etymologically, the name derives from the Hebrew "*adamah*" (red earth), since "the LORD God formed man out of the clay of the ground" (Gn 2:7).

Noah
Prompted by God, he builds an ark in which his family and one pair of every animal (Gn 6:19-20) take refuge during the great deluge. The Bible considers his three children (Shem, Ham, and Japheth) the progenitors of the human family.

Abraham
He is the father of the people of Israel, originally from Mesopotamia: perhaps Ur of Chaldea, near the lower course of the Euphrates River. He has two sons: Ishmael, from his slave Hagar; and at a later age Isaac, from his wife, Sarah. The Arabs consider him their father through Ishmael. He is called "our father in faith" by Christians. Abraham lived around 1400 BC.

Melchizedek

Priest-king of Salem (Jerusalem), he brings bread and wine to Abraham and blesses him. According to many scholars, the appearance of Melchizedek, which is isolated and mysterious (not even a general description is provided in the biblical account), prefigures the kingly priesthood of Christ.

Isaac

Abraham is one hundred years old and Sarah is ninety years old when Isaac is born. The second patriarch of Israel, Isaac is remembered because God, in order to test Abraham's faith, asks Abraham to sacrifice his son Isaac. Then God himself miraculously provides the victim for the burnt offering, saving the child.

Rebekah

Only after twenty years of waiting is her marriage to Isaac blessed by the arrival of twins: Esau and Jacob. Esau exchanges his birthright for a bowl of stew, and Rebekah shrewdly obtains Isaac's blessing for Jacob instead.

Jacob

The son of Isaac and Rebekah, he is an astute and strategic person. Though tricked into marrying Leah, he marries her sister Rachel as well. The name "Israel," which God assigns to him, becomes the name of the nation: the twelve tribes of Israel all descend from the children and grandchildren of Jacob. He is one of the most important individuals in Jewish history, and his name is cited in the Bible more often than Abraham's.

Joseph

The son of Jacob and Rachel, Joseph evokes the jealousy of his brothers and is sold by them as a slave in Egypt. He shows that he is a capable and wise person and is able to interpret Pharaoh's dreams. Because of this, he becomes the viceroy. His tomb is still marked today by a building near Jacob's well, near Nablus in Israel.

Moses

The Old Testament attributes to him the role of guidance in Israel's exodus from Egypt. He probably lived in the time of Pharaoh Ramses II (1301-1234 BC). Born in Egypt to Jewish parents, he is miraculously saved from death and raised in the court of the pharaoh. In the desert of Midian, where he flees after killing an Egyptian, he receives his call from the Eternal

God. He leads the Chosen People out of Egypt on a journey that lasts forty years. On Mount Horeb (also called Sinai), he establishes the Old Covenant with the Almighty and receives the Ten Commandments. He dies on Mount Nebo, contemplating the Promised Land without being able to enter it.

Joshua

While Moses sings praise for the blessings he has received and prepares himself for death, Joshua leads the children of Israel into the Promised Land. The Book of Joshua describes the conquest and distribution of the territory among the twelve tribes. The Battle of Jericho, perhaps the most famous conflict in the entire Bible, is Joshua's first victory.

Samson

The Book of Judges recounts the feats of Samson, who puts his strength at the service of Israel in its conflict against the Philistines. The secret of his strength—his long hair—is revealed to Delilah, his Philistine lover, who betrays him by handing him over to his enemies. Taken prisoner, he is chained between the central columns of the Philistines' temple and uses his strength to make the building collapse.

Ruth

A foreign woman belonging to the Moabites (a people often in conflict with Israel), Ruth harbors a tender pity toward her Jewish mother-in-law, Naomi. Left a widow, she takes Naomi back to her native Bethlehem, where Ruth marries Boaz and becomes the grandmother of King David, thereby becoming part of Christ's family tree. For this reason, she is mentioned by Matthew at the beginning of his Gospel.

Saul

The first king of Israel, Saul fights against the Ammonites and the Philistines, but he goes from being humble to prideful. Tormented by melancholy and fears of persecution, he is calmed by the harp of young David. In old age, jealous of David's growing popularity, he tries several times to kill the future king. He takes his own life by falling on his sword.

David

As a boy, he kills the giant Goliath armed only with a sling. Having become the second king of Israel, he expands the kingdom through numerous victories over the Philistines and Moabites. He establishes the capital city in Jerusalem and becomes the ideal just king. He turns to God at tumultuous moments in his life, composing numerous psalms expressing sincere repentance for his faults.

Solomon

David chooses Solomon, his son with Bathsheba, to succeed him to the throne. Solomon begins the construction of the great Temple of Jerusalem and extends the kingdom, expanding commerce by land and sea. His reputation as a wise man reaches the Queen of Sheba, who comes to visit him. However, in his later years, through the influence of his foreign wives, he strays from his dedication to the one true God. After his death, the kingdom divides into the kingdoms of Israel and Judah.

Elijah

The greatest of all the Prophets, Elijah prophesied in Judah for forty years without leaving any writings. The First Book of Kings recounts his career as a prophet. On Mount Carmel, he shows that Yahweh, not Baal, is the true God. Threatened by Queen Jezebel, he flees to the desert and reaches Mount Horeb: here, the Lord speaks to him in "a tiny whispering sound" (1 Kgs 19:12). Near the desert of Damascus he encounters Elisha, who follows him. He is lifted up to heaven in a chariot of fire, leading to the belief that Elijah did not die but often returns to the earth. In this light, it is easier to understand the scornful statement that was reportedly made at the foot of Jesus' Cross: "wait, let us see if Elijah comes to save him" (Mt 27:49).

Tobiah

Tobiah's story takes place during the period of the Babylonian exile. Tobiah's father, Tobit, goes blind while resting after piously burying his dead kinsman. But God, responding to their prayers, sends the Angel Raphael in the guise of a young man, who tells Tobiah to restore Tobit's vision by anointing his eyes with fish gall.

Judith

A beautiful, God-fearing Jewish woman, Judith lived during the time of the Assyrian king Nebuchadnezzar. Earning the trust of Holofernes, the head of the Assyrian army, she is invited to a banquet in his honor. When the Assyrian commander becomes drunk, she decapitates him, thereby liberating the people of Israel.

Esther

This Jewish exile attracts the attention of the Persian king Ahasuerus, who marries her. Having learned of a plan by the vizier, Haman, to exterminate the Jews, she reveals the plot to the king. Haman is then condemned to death, and his position as vizier is given to Mordecai, Esther's foster-father. The Jews, originally destined to be eliminated, are authorized to take vengeance and kill 75,000 men. The Jewish feast of Purim commemorates these events.

Job

A rich and influential man who is presented as a perfect believer, Job becomes the object of a curious bet between God and Satan to determine if Job's faith will waver if he loses his material success. Despite being derided by his friends and relatives, and struggling with profound inner turmoil, he patiently bears multiple adversities by maintaining faith in the triumph of justice over evil.

Isaiah

This prophet lived in Jerusalem during the eighth century BC. A collection of prophecies, written under great poetic inspiration and traceable to several authors, were handed down under his name. The most famous prophecy is the announcement of the Messiah: "the virgin shall be with child, and bear a son, and shall name him Immanuel" (Is 7:14).

Jeremiah

Jeremiah is called by God himself to become a prophet. He resists the call, since he feels he lacks the necessary gifts, and accepts only when the Lord, lightly brushing his mouth, promises to stay by his side. Ignored by the inhabitants of Judah, he predicts the destruction of Jerusalem, which occurs in 587 BC at the hands of Nebuchadnezzar, king of Babylon.

Ezekiel

Ezekiel is the first prophet of Israel to work outside its borders, writing his book during the exile in Babylon. In one of his visions of the glory of the Lord, the figures of four beings appear—man, lion, bull, and eagle—which some people have associated with the symbols of the four evangelists.

Daniel

Daniel is a young Jew who is deported to Babylon and is taught in the court of the king. He is respected for his ability to interpret dreams, and—after many events—he is assigned the office of governor of the city. The story of Susanna, saved from being stoned thanks to the cleverness of Daniel, is passed down in this book.

Jonah

This prophet receives from God the task of preaching repentance in the city of Nineveh, which is inhabited by the Assyrians, enemies of the Hebrew people. But he flees on a boat headed in the opposite direction. Tossed into the sea, he is saved by God through the miracle of the large fish that swallows him and returns him to dry land after three days. At that point, Jonah obeys and fulfills the mission entrusted to him.

Jesus

Christianity is founded on the person of Jesus, the Son of the living God and the Redeemer of humanity. The name "Jesus" means "Yahweh is salvation." The life, works, and message of Jesus are testified to in the New Testament, especially in the Gospels, the Acts of the Apostles, and the letters of St. Paul. Roman historians Flavius Josephus, Pliny the Younger, Tacitus, and Suetonius also speak of Jesus. Jesus was a historical person, even though it is impossible to know the dates of his birth and death with certainty. The evangelists were not concerned with providing a historical-biographical report. For them, it was necessary to affirm the universal importance of the incarnation of Jesus, the Messiah eagerly awaited by all peoples.

Gabriel

The plentiful gospel evidence for the divine nature of Jesus begins with the account of the miracle of the Annunciation: the appearance of the Archangel Gabriel to the Virgin Mary in Nazareth (see Lk 1:26-38). Gabriel does not greet Mary with her proper name, but rather calls her "full of grace," or "filled by God with grace," or "favored one," a title intended to signify the fullness of God's love for her.

The Magi

Coming from the east to find the newborn King of the Jews, the Magi reach Bethlehem guided by a star. As recorded in the Gospel of Matthew, "on entering the house they saw the child with Mary his mother. They prostrated themselves and did him homage" (Mt 2:11). A later tradition attributes to them the names of Balthasar, Melchior, and Caspar.

Mary

The biblical information on the Mother of Jesus comes from the Gospels according to Matthew, Luke, and John. In the Gospel of Matthew, we learn of the visit of the Magi and the flight into Egypt. In the Gospel of Luke, we find the accounts of the Annunciation, the visit to Elizabeth (during which Mary thanks God in the *Magnificat*), the birth of the Redeemer in Bethlehem, the presentation of the Son at the Temple, and the losing and finding of twelve-year-old Jesus in the Temple in Jerusalem. In the Gospel of John, Mary is present at the wedding at Cana and at the foot of the Cross, when Christ entrusts her to his beloved disciple. Mary is again mentioned in the Acts of the Apostles, when she receives the Holy Spirit together with the Apostles. The Virgin—who "kept all these things, reflecting on them in her heart" (Lk 2:19)— was always held in very special regard by the Christian community.

Joseph

The husband of Mary, foster-father of Jesus, and head of the Holy Family, Joseph links the Messiah to the house of David. Enlightened by an angel about the nature of Mary's pregnancy (Mt 1:18-25), he is present at the birth of the Redeemer in Bethlehem and at the presentation in the Temple. After the flight into Egypt, he establishes their home in Nazareth, where he works as a carpenter and is assisted by Jesus in this manual labor.

John the Baptist

The son of Zechariah and Elizabeth, John the Baptist lives in solitude in the desert, eating locusts and honey (see Mk 1:2-15). A preacher of repentance, he appears in all of the Gospels and baptizes Jesus at the beginning of Jesus' public life. He opposes the adultery of Herod Antipas who, at the behest of his lover Herodias, has the Baptist beheaded.

Matthew

Also known as Levi, Jesus calls him from his work as a tax collector to become one of the Twelve. The Gospel that bears his name is rich with details about the teachings of Jesus. It was one of the most heavily used sacred books during the time of early Christianity. The first intended recipients of this Gospel were Christians of Jewish origin.

Mark

The oldest and shortest of the Gospels is attributed to Mark, a cousin of Barnabas and companion of Paul. His Gospel was probably written for the Christians in Rome after the deaths of Peter and Paul. The Gospel of Mark, which Matthew and Luke likely drew on, was written for believers who converted from paganism. The text is rich with specific annotations about the person of Jesus, who is presented as a sensible and courageous man, even in challenging certain Jewish traditions. The aim of his teaching is to guide humanity to the faith.

Luke

A companion of Paul, probably from Antioch (where the appellative "Christian" was used for the first time), Luke is a highly cultured physician who writes in pristine Greek, as his Gospel and the Acts of the Apostles demonstrate. Particularly interested in the birth and childhood of Jesus, he provides the most complete account of the life of the Redeemer, giving much attention to Mary, whom Luke seems to consider the most important and distinguished biblical person after Jesus. In the many parables that Luke recounts, he seeks above all to illuminate the bountiful mercy of Christ.

John

A son of the fisherman Zebedee, John and his brother James together receive the nickname "sons of thunder" for their impulsiveness. Among the first of those who are called, he is the beloved disciple: seated close to Jesus during the Last Supper, he remains with Mary at the foot of the Cross and believes in the Resurrection when he sees the empty tomb. The expression "I am the way and the truth and the life" (Jn 14:6) is found only in his Gospel.

Peter

A fisherman from Capernaum, on the Sea of Galilee (also called the Lake of Gennesaret), Peter is the brother of Andrew. Named Simon, he is renamed by Jesus with the symbolic name of Peter, indicating his function as the rock on which the Church is built. For his recognition of Jesus as the Christ, he receives the reward of primacy among the Twelve Apostles (see Mt 16:13-19). At the moment of Christ's capture, he strikes the servant of the high priest; shortly thereafter, he denies his Master three times. Immediately afterward, Peter repents and cries bitter tears. The Acts of the Apostles assigns Peter a preeminent role in the early Church. He dies in Rome under Nero, crucified—according to tradition—upside down.

Paul

A Roman citizen originally named Saul, Paul is born in Tarsus in Cilicia and is a strictly-practicing Jew of the Tribe of Benjamin. He studies law in Jerusalem and becomes a harsh persecutor of the early Christians, present during the stoning of Stephen, the first martyr (see Acts 7:54-60). Experiencing a conversion on the road to Damascus, he dedicates his life to evangelization with tireless zeal. After many journeys, he is killed by beheading in Rome under Nero.

The Spouses at Cana

"There was a wedding in Cana in Galilee, and the mother of Jesus was there. Jesus and his disciples were also invited to the wedding" (Jn 2:1). In order to save the spouses the embarrassment of running out of wine during the banquet, Jesus—thanks to Mary's farsighted intercession—performs his first miracle by turning water into wine. The servants fill six jars "to the brim," or to their maximum capacity, and Jesus provides abundant wine as his first sign.

The Paralytic

Jesus says to him, "Rise, pick up your stretcher, and go home" (Mt 9:6). The Redeemer performs a physical healing to show that spiritual healing—forgiveness of sins—is just as real: the man "rose and went home" (Mt 9:7). The event occurs in Capernaum, a little city presented as Jesus' official place of residence: "his own town" (Mt 9:1).

Mary Magdalene

Originally from Magdala, a small town on the Sea of Galilee, Mary Magdalene is freed of seven demons and becomes a disciple of the Teacher (see Lk 8:2). She is mentioned by the four Gospels, together with other women, as being part of Jesus' itinerant group. She is present at the Crucifixion and is the first person to whom the Risen Christ appears (see Jn 20:1-18).

The Hemorrhaging Woman

This anonymous woman, suffering from chronic hemorrhages, comes up behind Jesus and touches the tassel of his cloak (see Mt 9:20-22). The Teacher, who feels strength go out of him, finds her in the crowd and tells her, "Courage, daughter! Your faith has saved you" (Mt 9:22). At that moment, the woman is cured.

The Canaanite Woman

This woman from the region of Tyre and Sidon asks for help for her sick daughter, despite living in a pagan land. At first, Jesus does not listen to her because he does not consider it right to take bread from the children (the Jews) to give it to the dogs (the pagans). The Canaanite woman (see Mt 15:27) notes that even the dogs feed on the scraps that fall from the table. Seeing her faith, Jesus heals her daughter.

The Samaritan Woman

Jesus meets the Samaritan woman at the well in Sychar (see Jn 4:5-30) and says to her, "Give me a drink." Since the Samaritans are not recognized as true Jews by the authorities of Jerusalem, the woman is amazed by the fact that a Jew would ask her for a drink. Jesus presents himself as the giver of living water—the Holy Spirit—and tells her, "If you knew the gift of God and who is saying to you, 'Give me a drink,' you would have asked him and he would have given you living water" (Jn 4:10). The woman understands that Jesus is the Messiah and announces it to the people in the city.

The Boy with the Loaves and Fish

The crowd following Jesus becomes hungry, and Jesus realizes it and asks the disciples to provide the necessary food. The Apostle Andrew indicates a boy who "has five barley loaves and two fish" (Jn 6:9), and with these Jesus performs the miracle of the multiplication of the loaves. After having satisfied the hunger of the crowd, the Teacher begins the sermon on the Bread of Life.

The Leper

Considered untouchable by the Jews, a leper comes up to Jesus and prostrates himself before him: "Lord, if you wish, you can make me clean" (Mt 8:2). Jesus could heal him with a look or a word. Instead, he extends his hand and touches him, and says, "I will do it. Be made clean" (Mt 8:3). And his leprosy immediately disappears.

The Blind Man

He is healed when Christ, "the light of the world" (Jn 9:5), smears his eyes with clay, made from dirt and saliva (see Jn 9:1-12). The fact that the man has been blind from birth leads the disciples to ask Jesus about whose guilt the blindness punishes: that of the blind man or of his parents. For the Lord, illness is not a punishment inflicted for sins but rather can become the occasion for salvation and God's Revelation.

The Widow of Nain

"When the Lord saw her, he was moved with pity for her and said to her, 'Do not weep'" (Lk 7:13). The miracle of the resurrection of the son of the widow happens in Nain, through these firm words: "Young man, I tell you, arise!" (Lk 7:14). Jesus once again proves himself as the Lord over life and death.

Martha and Mary

These sisters live in Bethany with their brother Lazarus and are friends of Jesus. During one of his visits, Martha continues to concern herself with all of the domestic chores while Mary instead sits and listens to their guest. When Martha complains that she has been left alone in serving, Jesus tells her that there is only need of one thing and that Mary has chosen the better part (see Lk 10:38-42).

Lazarus

One of the three resurrections performed by Jesus (the others are of Jairus' daughter and the son of the widow of Nain) happens in Bethany, a small village near Jerusalem. Lazarus falls ill, and his sisters, Martha and Mary, call Jesus. He arrives after Lazarus has been dead for four days. Jesus bursts into tears, prays to the Father, and then performs the miracle: "Lazarus, come out!" (Jn 11:43). "Now many of the Jews who had come to Mary and seen what he had done began to believe in him" (Jn 11:45).

Zacchaeus

The chief tax collector of Jericho, Zacchaeus leads a comfortable life wringing money out of the Judeans to pay the Roman taxes. Being short in stature and curious about Jesus, he climbs a sycamore tree when Jesus is passing by (see Lk 19:1-10). Struck by the Lord's words—"Zacchaeus, come down quickly, for today I must stay at your house" (Lk 19:5)—he decides to become a new man.

Judas

"While he was still speaking, a crowd approached and in front was one of the Twelve, a man named Judas. He went up to Jesus to kiss him. Jesus said to him, 'Judas, are you betraying the Son of Man with a kiss?'" (Lk 22:47-48). The betrayer, who is scandalized by the waste of money on the perfume that Mary of Bethany used to anoint the feet of Jesus, has already been designated a "thief" by John, after he stole from the shared money bag (see Jn 12:6). Jesus nonetheless calls him "friend" (Mt 26:50).

Pilate

Pilate is the Roman prefect of the province of Judea, whose existence is historically verified even by non-biblical sources. During Jesus' trial, Pilate finds no grounds for condemning him. But he "washe[s] his hands in the sight of the crowd, saying, 'I am innocent of this man's blood. Look to it yourselves'" (Mt 27:24). And he hands Jesus over "to be crucified" (Mt 27:26).

Simon of Cyrene

"They pressed into service a passer-by, Simon, a Cyrenian, who was coming in from the country, the father of Alexander and Rufus, to carry his cross" (Mk 15:21). Mark, who rarely makes citations, indicates the names of the children of the Cyrenian: a fact that perhaps means that they were well known in the community he was addressing (see Rm 16:13).

The Centurion

The centurion's confession at the foot of the Cross, together with the others who were keeping watch over Jesus with him, is the most genuine profession of faith: "truly, this was the Son of God!" (Mt 27:54). It is the profession of someone who believes during the darkest moments of life.

Thomas

One of the Twelve, Thomas is known for his unbelief. "Jesus came, although the doors were locked, and stood in their midst and said, 'Peace be with you.' Then he said to Thomas, 'Put your finger here and see my hands, and bring your hand and put it into my side, and do not be unbelieving, but believe.' . . . 'Blessed are those who have not seen and have believed'" (Jn 20:26-29).

Stephen

Known as "a man filled with faith and the holy Spirit" (Acts 6:5), Stephen was appointed to assist the Twelve in serving the early Christian community. He preached the Gospel of Jesus Christ boldly and worked great signs in Jerusalem, stirring up charges of blasphemy. Tried before the Sanhedrin, he became the first martyr, forgiving his killers and commending his spirit to God.

4. HOW TO READ THE BIBLE

- Faith in the Word of God
- The living Tradition of the Word of God
- Interpretation of the literal meaning
- Historical-cultural context
- Integrity of the content

he reading of Sacred Scripture—as with every area of knowledge—must be approached with sufficient preparation. A **proper understanding of the Bible** calls for certain **interpretive requirements,** which are listed as follows.

Faith in the Word of God

To open the Bible is to enter into the mystery of loving communication with God.

The history of this event (history of salvation)—with the **person of Jesus Christ, the Incarnate Word**, at its center—is communicated to us by means of **two sources: Tradition and the Sacred Scriptures**. "Sacred Tradition and sacred Scripture . . . are bound closely together, and communicate one with the other. . . . Hence, both Scripture and Tradition must be accepted and honored with equal feelings of devotion and reverence" (DV, no. 9).

God first manifests himself through *Revelation*, by which he begins the history of salvation, then through the *Incarnation*, in which he becomes man and accomplishes the salvation of humanity. This is the **essential event**, the living truth, that needs to be accepted in life. *Every person can freely trust or not trust, believe or not believe, in the Word of God.* This is the dramatic and tremendous existential decision of every person.

Faith means believing in God who speaks and believing in God who loves.

The whole Bible, as St. Augustine said, does nothing other than "tell the love of God."[2]

---

2 *The Augustine Catechism: The Enchiridion of Faith, Hope, and Love*, 1:84. Quotation translated from the Italian.

Furthermore, before "faith can be exercised, man must have the grace of God to move and assist him; he must have the interior helps of the Holy Spirit, who moves the heart and converts it to God, who opens the eyes of the mind" (DV, no. 5).

The first fundamental element for reading the Bible is, therefore, the ability to make room for the action of the Holy Spirit, who "constantly perfects faith by his gifts" (DV, no. 5).

The Living Tradition of the Word of God

The Old Testament emerged from oral traditions. In the ancient world, great weight was placed on the spoken word. The greatest of all the Prophets, Elijah, as well as Isaiah and others, did not leave any writings.

Jesus himself entrusted his Gospel to the community of the Apostles orally, that is, by speaking.

In the New Testament, the Tradition is an essential part of the apostolic witness concerning Jesus. "Tradition transmits in its entirety the Word of God which has been entrusted to the apostles by Christ the Lord and the Holy Spirit. It transmits it to the successors of the apostles" (DV, no. 9).

During the time of the persecutions, believers were required to hand over the Sacred Books so that the roots of the faith could be destroyed.

Interpretation of the Literal Meaning

 hen one reads the Bible, it is critical to **discern the authentic literal meaning** in order to seek the "meaning which God had thought well to manifest through the medium of their [the sacred writers'] words" (DV, no. 12), and not to fall into interpretations that are erroneous and dangerous to the faith. The "literal meaning" is the meaning intended by the author as conveyed in the actual text.

"The task of giving an authentic interpretation of the Word of God, whether in its written form or in the form of Tradition, has been entrusted to the living teaching office of the Church alone. Its authority in this matter is exercised in the name of Jesus Christ" (DV, no. 10).

> Ye have the Old and the New Testament
> And the Pastor of the Church who guideth you:
> Let this suffice you unto your salvation.
> (Dante, *Paradiso* V:76-78 [trans. Longfellow])

It is essential for Christians to have a good version of the Bible in order to become familiar with reading the Word of God carefully, through the aid of a text with clear and trustworthy explanatory notes. In the United States, the *New American Bible* is most commonly used in worship and catechesis. Catholics may use any translation bearing an *imprimatur* for private devotion and study.

Historical-Cultural Context

he seventy-three books that make up the Bible were written during a timespan lasting from roughly 900 BC to AD 100.

Various cultures became intertwined during those years. As a result, the message of the history of salvation has been transmitted through **various modes of expression**: historical accounts, parables, didactic stories, poetic texts, idiomatic expressions, hymns, prayers, speeches, letters, family histories, slang expressions, and more. **Literary genres**, such as these, are different ways to express thought; they vary in their tone, content, and style. (See the sidebar "Senses of Scripture.")

When one reads the Bible, it is very important to research and identify the different forms of these texts. For "'truth is differently presented and expressed in the various types of historical writing, in prophetical and poetical texts,' and in other forms of literary expression" (DV, no. 12).

Senses of Scripture

The *United States Catholic Catechism for Adults* describes ways to understand the meaning of Scripture:

> The Church recognizes two senses of Scripture, the literal and the spiritual. In probing the literal meaning of the texts, it is necessary to determine their literary form, such as history, hymns, wisdom sayings, poetry, parable, or other forms of figurative language. "The *literal sense* is the meaning conveyed by the words of Scripture and discovered by exegesis [the process scholars use to determine the meaning of the text], following the rules of sound interpretation: 'All other senses of Sacred Scripture are based on the literal'" (*Catechism of the Catholic Church*, no. 116, citing St. Thomas Aquinas, *Summa Theologiae* I, 1, 10).
>
> The spiritual senses of Sacred Scripture derive from the unity of God's plan of salvation. The text of Scripture discloses God's plan. The realities and events of which it speaks can also be signs of the divine plan. There are three spiritual senses of Scripture:
>
> > "1. The *allegorical sense*. We can acquire a more profound understanding of events by recognizing their significance in Christ; thus the crossing of the Red Sea is a sign or type of Christ's victory over sin and also of Christian Baptism.

"2. The *moral sense*. The events reported in Scripture ought to lead us to act justly. As St. Paul says, they were written 'for our instruction' (1 Cor 10:11).

"3. The *anagogical sense*. . . . We can view realities and events in terms of their eternal significance, leading us toward our true homeland: thus the Church on earth is a sign of the heavenly Jerusalem."*

---

* *United States Catholic Catechism for Adults* (Washington, DC: USCCB, 2006), 27-28, citing *Catechism of the Catholic Church* (Washington, DC: Libreria Editrice Vaticana–USCCB, 2000), nos. 116, 117.

Integrity of the Content

he unity of the plan of salvation requires every passage of the Bible to be compared with others, **in harmony with the whole of the content**. Serious attention "must be devoted to the content and unity of the whole of Scripture . . . if we are to derive their true meaning from the sacred texts" (DV, no. 12).

This unity not only sheds light on the interpretation of the New Testament as a whole, but it also has repercussions for the evaluation of the texts of the Old Testament in the perspective of the history of salvation.

Pope Benedict calls this way of reading the Bible "**canonical exegesis**," the practice of reading and interpreting Scripture in its unity, as a single work leading to the Revelation of God in Christ. As the Holy Father explains, "Scripture . . . can only be properly understood if [it is] read . . . as a oneness in which there is progress towards Christ, and inversely, in which Christ draws all history to himself; and if, moreover, all this is brought to life in the Church's faith" (Address to the bishops of Switzerland, November 7, 2006).

"Thus 'all Scripture is inspired by God, and profitable for teaching, for reproof, for correction and for training in righteousness, so that the man of God may be complete, equipped for every good work' (2 Tm 3:16-17, Greek text)" (DV, no. 11).

Therefore, all the books of the Bible should be read in the context of a **harmonious and comprehensive perspective**, which is the history of salvation.

The numerous writings of the Bible are not simply pieces of tile placed in a static mosaic; rather, they are bound to the dynamic unity of the **path leading to the historical event of Christ the Redeemer**. Similarly, it is not appropriate to take individual verses out of context without seeing how they relate to the literary work from which they were drawn.

"When the fullness of time had come," says St. Paul, "God sent his Son" (Gal 4:4-5).

Challenging Pages

"There are more than a few challenging pages of the Bible: after more than twenty years of passionate research, sustained by faith or simply by respect for the most venerated book in all of world literature, many things have been clarified, but not everything."*

Historical and scientific references, episodes of violence and war, or harsh and desperate language leave the reader very surprised. The key to understanding these pages is found in the commentary texts. The objective is to recount the mystery of the history of salvation and not to propose a manual of science, history, anthropology, or social doctrine.

---

* F. Galbiati and A. Piazza, *Pagine Difficili della Bibbia* [*Challenging Pages of the Bible*] (Milan, 1985). Quotation translated from the Italian.

5. THE MESSAGE OF THE BIBLE

- Biblical revival
- Biblical approaches
- The Bible and the liturgy
- The Bible, code of Christian life

Biblical Revival

It is easy to confirm how, in modern society, the agonizing search for *earthly things*, the withering of faith in the Risen Christ, and the weakening of the sense of morality make the message of the Bible increasingly difficult to accept.

And if it is true that there is no other work available in so many languages—about 2,500—as the Bible is, then one could estimate that only half of the 6 billion people in the world are unaware of its existence.

Today, the **biblical revival** is authentic, particularly in the Church, since for many believers the Bible, the Book of Books, becomes the interpretive key for understanding the meaning of history and of one's own life.

The Bible recounts the most divergent realities—those of light and of shadows—of the human race. It proclaims that God loves not only an orderly and honest world, but also the world as it is, corrupted by human beings, who can abuse their freedom.

To humankind, which needs hope and certitude, the **biblical** message offers the incredible possibility of an encounter between human misery and that patient, merciful, divine goodness, revealing the loving plan contained in the story of salvation.

Biblical Approaches

n the sacred books the Father who is in heaven comes lovingly to meet his children, and talks with them" (DV, no. 21). This is stated in the books that recount the history of Israel and also in those of the New Testament.

In a direct approach to Sacred Scripture, it is imperative that an interpretation influenced by old, rationalistic tendencies—contrary to the objective, historical reality of the Bible—be set aside. It is likewise necessary to set aside an uncritical—fundamentalist, subjective, or imaginative—interpretation, far removed from the concrete concerns of life.

The authentic approach to the essence of the Bible sheds light on the contemporary person's great existential and religious questions, and it helps one to live in the community in the dignity of one's own person.

For this reason, believers plan to **keep the Bible on hand** and reverently listen to the Word of God (see DV, no. 1), imitating Mary who hears and observes it (see Lk 10:39, 11:27). St. Francis wanted the Gospel to be lived to the letter, *sine glossa*, that is, without reductive commentary or convenient manipulation.

In the Bible, Christians discover God's plan for the world and live the Word as "food for the soul, and a pure and lasting fount of spiritual life" (DV, no. 21).

The Bible and the Liturgy

very liturgical rite (including the Mass, the other sacraments, and the Liturgy of the Hours) includes the proclamation of biblical readings. The liturgical texts themselves—orations, exhortations, and blessings—draw from the Scriptures, too; particular images, sayings, and expressions often are quoted directly from biblical texts. For example, the first words of the *Gloria* echo the angels in Luke 2:14, and the *Sanctus* quotes Isaiah 6. The Book of Psalms, the first prayer book of the Church, has always been a source of the language of liturgical prayer.

The liturgical reforms of the Second Vatican Council expanded use of the Scriptures in the liturgy. The *Constitution on the Sacred Liturgy* (*Sacrosanctum Concilium* [SC]) said that "the treasures of the Bible are to be opened up more lavishly so that a richer fare may be provided for the faithful at the table of God's word" (SC, no. 51). The result was the expansion of the cycle of Scripture readings, as well as the addition of readings from the Old Testament.

In the celebration of Mass on Sundays and solemnities, three readings from Scripture are proclaimed (not counting the Psalm, which is a part of the proclaimed Word of God, although it is normally sung in part by the liturgical assembly): (1) a reading from the Old Testament (except during the Easter Season, when the first reading is taken from the Acts of the Apostles); (2) a reading from one of the New Testament letters or the Book of Revelation; and (3) a reading from the Gospel. On weekdays, two readings are used, selected in semi-continuous fashion (that is, using large excerpts that continue from one day to the next): the first is either from the Old Testament or the New Testament, and the second is from the Gospel.

The guiding principle for the selection of the readings on Sundays and feast days is the principle of harmony. The texts complement one another thematically, usually centering on the reading from the Gospel. In particular, the Old Testament readings anticipate or reflect the event or theme of the day's Gospel or the feast. The harmony of these texts demonstrates what Catholics believe about the Bible, about Jesus, and about the relationship between the Old and New Testaments. Namely, the context of salvation history is Jesus; and the Old Testament, as it depicts the unfolding of God's creation, covenant, and relationship with his people, prepares for and leads to the coming of Christ in human history in his Incarnation in the flesh.

The Bible, Code of Christian Life

he community of believers, letting itself be permeated by the Word of God in the light of the Holy Spirit who inspired it, ultimately receives a further drive to live every day in accordance with the Gospel.

One might allude to a broad biblical range in which the Word of God, which is always alive and active, is capable of freeing hidden meanings and energies in response to new questions and situations.

The Word of God given in the Bible should have an impact on many facets of the Church's life:

- Theology
- Exegesis (study of Scripture)
- Liturgy
- Culture
- Diocesan and parochial spiritual life
- Personal prayer (*lectio divina*)
- Catechesis
- Ecclesial movements and associations
- Modern communications media
- Communities of consecrated life
- Life of the believer

- Family
- Bible studies
- Bible groups and guides
- Various aids (for example, collecting Bible passages for little children, older children, young adults, spouses, missions, suffering persons)

We can conclude by recalling the **centrality of the Word of God** in the words of *Dei Verbum*: "So may it come that, by the reading and study of the sacred books 'the Word of God may speed on and triumph' (2 Thes 3:1) and the treasure of Revelation entrusted to the Church may more and more fill the hearts of men. Just as from constant attendance at the eucharistic mystery the life of the Church draws increase, so a new impulse of spiritual life may be expected from increased veneration of the Word of God, which 'stands forever' (Is 40:8; see 1 Pt 1:23-25)" (DV, no. 26).

Lectio Divina

The expression "*lectio divina*" (reading of the Word of God), which is used in the Rule of St. Benedict (chapter 48), refers to an ancient method of personal or communal reading of a brief passage from Sacred Scripture. The method involves five steps:

- **Reading (*Lectio*)**. One reads and rereads the text with concentration and attention, correctly interpreting it and connecting it with other similar biblical texts.
- **Meditation (*Meditatio*)**. One applies the reading to one's personal life. A short phrase, dense with meaning, can be taken from the biblical text to guidethe whole day.
- **Prayer (*Oratio*)**. This is the moment of praise. One who prays should feel personally involved in honest and affectionate dialogue with God.
- **Contemplation (*Contemplatio*)**. This is the ability to let oneself be possessed by the Word. It is God who acts; a life-changing response is asked of us.
- **Action (*Actio*)**. "Blessed are those who hear the word of God and observe it" (Lk 11:28).